Dr Kit Bryson and
of several books that never quite made the grade, ranging from their blockbusting thriller *The Guns of Neasden Way* to various humour titles such as *101 Uses of a Dead Horse* and *The Book of Heroic Successes* (a slim autobiographical volume).

The authors would like to live in Oxford with the wife, three kids and a dog; they'd settle for a flat in Balham with the girlfriend and a budgie; they've got a bedsit in Hackney.

You Want, You'd Settle For, You Get

Dr Kit Bryson and Jean-Luc Legris

HEADLINE

First published in paperback in Great Britain in 1987
by HEADLINE BOOK PUBLISHING PLC

ISBN 0-7472-3018-8

Printed and bound in Great Britain by
Collins, Glasgow

HEADLINE BOOK PUBLISHING PLC
Headline House
79 Great Titchfield Street
London W1P 7FN

ONE

You want to be 18.
You'd settle for being 17.
You are 11.

You want a loving mother.

You'd settle for a mother who lives with your father.

You end up with a mother who leaves you sitting on a tuckbox at Waterloo Station with your feet not touching the ground. 'You won't mind if I don't wait, darling, I do so hate goodbyes.'

You want a father who comes to Sports Day in a Rolls-Royce and scores a century in the Father's Match.

You'd settle for a father who comes to Sports Day without your mother.

You end up with a father who brings your mother to Sports Day, and she wears a hat and takes her shoes off, and in the obstacle race they get stuck in a drain.

You want a polka-dot bikini.

You'd settle for a swirly skirt with Red Indians on it.

You end up in a green crimplene dress and an Easter bonnet.

You want to fall over in the playground so that Mr. Andrews will give you the kiss of life.

You'd settle for him smiling at you at the school dance.

You end up with him saying, 'Take that fake fur off for heaven's sake, this is a school dance not a fancy dress parade.'

You want to be tall and sleek so that Mr. Andrews will like you.

You'd settle for not being podgy.

You end up spilling your spotted dick and custard over your skirt so that you won't have to eat it and being made to stand in front of the whole school, and Mr. Andrews, in your grey school knickers.

You want a pony.

You'd settle for a poodle.

You get a tortoise that shits down your blouse when you pick it up.

You want parents who take you to a Tuscany farmhouse in August.

You'd settle for parents who take you for a dour two weeks in Gleneagles.

You end up packed off to a Pony Club in Wales so that your parents can walk around the house in the nude.

You wanted to be an aristocratic orphan left in the jungle and brought up by monkeys.

You'd have settled for being one of nine brothers brought up on the streets of Philadelphia by a drunken father called Bruno Kowalski.

You end up in Sunningdale with a father called Arthur Williamson, building nests in privet hedges and sitting in the branches of a melancholy yew tree.

You want a big brother to protect you.

You'd settle for a little sister you could dress up as a doll.

You end up with a big brother who makes you play doctors and nurses with a tray full of ice-cubes.

You want a big brother who'll beat up the bully down the road.

You'd settle for a twin so you could gang up on the bully down the road.

You get a little sister who laughs as the bully down the road beats you up.

You want to play the hero on a white charger.

You'd settle for being the cowboy with the red neckerchief and pistol.

You end up in the troop of Indians that gets massacred.

You want to go to Winchester.

You'd settle for going to Westminster.

You end up at Wellington.

On your first day at public school you want to impress the senior boys with your ancestral conkers and swimming certificate.

You'd settle for being inconspicuous and making a new friend.

You end up warming lavatory seats for prefects and being thrown out of windows by grown men.

You want to say, "You're all being horrid to Gibbens."

You'd settle for saying, "Do you want to walk with me, Gibbens?"

You end up saying, "Let's throw Gibbens out of a window."

You want to be top in English.

You'd settle for top in Religious Instruction.

You get a certificate for Best Kept Hamster.

You want to go over the line for the winning try with a bundle of boys and a broken rib.

You'd settle for playing an inconspicuous game in the second row of the scrum.

You end up missing a vital tackle in front of your mother and your sister and for 24 hours by medieval statute you're the boy everyone can punch up the stomach.

You want Catherine Deneuve.

You'd settle for Anne Bancroft.

You end up being kissed by your one-legged house-master.

You want the painfully beautiful girl you glimpsed on the platform at Bagshot Station.

You'd settle for your lumpy Canadian cousin.

You end up with a tart in Hogarth Place and she eats an apple while you do it.

You want to say, 'I did it with a tart in Hogarth Place. It was disgusting, Gibbens.'

You'd settle for saying, 'I did it, Gibbens, but it's actually rather over-rated.'

You say, 'Hey, I did it with my pretty Canadian cousin! It was great!'

You want to lose your virginity to a Second Lieutenant with tight trousers and a Porsche.

You'd settle for Caroline's brother, even though he goes to Harrow.

You end up in a car park in Playo D'Aro under a Catalan waiter, squeaking like new shoes.

You want to say, 'Ugh! Ugh! Ugh! It's horrid, and it hurts, and the gravel gets into your bra, and all that yuck! yuck! yuck! stuff sticks to the hair on your legs!'

You'd settle for saying, 'I only wish I'd saved myself for the man I'm going to marry.'

You end up saying, 'It's actually rather over-rated.'

You want to be called Huck.

You'd settle for being called Chuck.

You're called Humphrey.

You want to be called Solitaire.

You'd settle for being called Sapphire.

You're called Ruby.

TWO

Et in arcadia ego.

You want to revisit Brideshead.

You'd settle for being an Oxford undergraduate.

You end up on the wrong side of Folly Bridge in a two-up with rising damp, fibrositic carpets and a polystyrene wigstand with toothpicks in its eyeballs and a hundred airgun pellets gouging out its face.

You want to go to Magadalen.

You'd settle for Trinity.

You end up at Brasenose.

You want to get to King's.

You'd settle for Trinity.

You end up at Magdalene.

You want to be dark and scornful and known in betting shops.

You'd settle for being dark and sad and known in the better restaurants.

You end up dark and shy and known in the College Buttery.

You want an Attic affair with a Fellow of All Souls.

You'd settle for a homosexual affair with a poet.

You end up kissing a man with a moustache in an Indian restaurant.

You want to wear two hats.

You'd settle for being in two minds.

You end up two-faced, having lunch with Gibbens.

You want to be Daniel Topolski.

You'd settle for stroking Oxford to victory.

You end up as a member of the Cambridge eight sinking in the grey scum of the Thames.

You want to say, 'Fuck this for a game of soldiers.'

You'd settle for saying, 'Sod this for a canary. I'm wet through and I want to go home.'

You end up saying, 'Next year we're in with a real chance. The pressure will all be on Oxford.'

You wish you'd gone to Oxford or Cambridge.

You'd settle for having gone to Durham or Bristol.

You end up saying, 'I pride myself on having a First in Common Sense from the University of Real Life.'

You want to be Roy Jenkins.

You'd settle for being Alf Dubs.

You end up as Norman Tebbit.

You want to teach your parents not to say 'toilet'.

You'd settle for not saying 'toilet' yourself.

You end up as Roy Jenkins.

You want to write musicals, publish poems, wear clothes, keep a pig's head on your mantlepiece, and have a column in The Sunday Times before your finals.

You'd settle for writing reviews, acting in sketches, a Third in English and a job with the BBC.

You get sent down for getting drunk, breaking a window, stealing a dressing-gown and beating up bull-dogs.

You want to entertain a doe-eyed girl from London with long legs and twinkling feet, and take her beagling.

You'd settle for dinner in an Indian restaurant with the girl who understudied Portia in a college production.

You end up drinking Nescafé with a common girl in a student scarf hoping she doesn't do it.

THREE

I count life just a stuff
To try the soul's strength on

Robert Browning

You want a job.

You'd settle for work.

You end up on Supplementary Benefit.

You want to live with artists and writers and disinherited marquesses in an abandoned squat in Thurloe Square.

You'd settle for living in a converted warehouse with a Vietnamese stocking model.

You end up living with Gibbens in Parson's Green.

You want to travel round Africa in a Winnebago with a girl and a gun.

You'd settle for going round Spain in a Dormobile.

You end up in a mobile home on the forecourt of a petrol station shooting pigeons with an air rifle and doing your washing in a bucket.

You want to live in a flat owned by your Daddy, with four girls, and when the phone rings everyone shrieks.

You'd settle for living in Daddy's basement but you can't because Daddy hasn't got a basement.

You end up sharing a bedroom with four other girls who put their names on their yoghurt.

You want to move smoothly through a seething street-life, at ease with its low glamour and hidden violence.

You'd settle for shouting boisterously at your friends across the street.

You end up holding shop doors open for Negroes.

You want to dance her smoothly into doorways and crush yourself against her.

You'd settle for dancing smoothly across the street to meet her.

You end up dancing smoothly across the street to meet her and going down in a puddle, legs spread like nut-crackers.

You want to say, 'Waiter! This wine is corked!'

You'd settle for saying, 'Waiter, I think you'd better taste this yourself, actually.'

You end up saying, 'Ah, perfect, it's delicious, thank you sir.'

You want to mix with musicians and drug addicts and write a blockbusting chronicle about them and their blonde, nihilistic women.

You'd settle for supplying pipes and papers to musicians and addicts at 4 per cent over cost.

You end up making two million out of mail-order and living with a Volvo in Gloucestershire, playing golf.

You want to be Arnold Schwarzenegger.

You'd settle for being taller than average.

You end up in cuban heels and padded shoulders.

You want to launch a national humour magazine to put *Private Eye* out of business.

You'd settle for a job on *Private Eye*.

You end up as the Entertainments Editor of *The Mail on Sunday*.

You wanted to be a Falklands hero.

You'd have settled for being an unsung hero.

You end up being blown to bits by a Sea Cat missile, and your parents get a bill for the damage.

You want to be a singer in the band.

You'd settle for singing in the bath.

You end up in a tube car, moaning along to your Walkman, hitting three notes out of five and changing key every two bars.

You want to die naked in a fast car with Jim Morrison on the tapedeck.

You'd settle for driving a Kawaski up the M1 at 120 mph with a blonde in black leather on the back.

You end up after a traffic accident in a brain-damage ward, drooling and moaning and rolling off your bed pan.

You want to be a deb of the year.

You'd settle for lurching gawkily down the catwalk at the Berkeley Dress Show.

You end up at the Berkeley Square Ball freebasing up a tree with Jamie Blandford.

You want to cease upon the midnight with no pain.

You'd settle for playing Russian roulette with a double barrelled shotgun.

You end up as a drug addict, stealing your sister's jewelry and responding to all criticism with a sad expression, 'Ah yes, but you see, I'm a junkie.'

You want to talk to an analyst.

You'd settle for talking to a friend.

You end up in group therapy defecating into a bucket in front of a roomful of strangers.

You want her to wear boots and a corset and act out the slave scene in *Spartacus*.

You'd settle for her talking about her lesbian experiences at school.

She climbs under the bedclothes, and after 10 minutes pudging away she says, 'Are you going to the Drinkwater's this weekend?'

You wanted to be a rock.

You'd settle for being a pillar.

You end up as a brick, married to Prince Andrew.

You wanted to show your legs on television.

You settled for marrying the Prince of Wales.

You end up being reprimanded in the great echoing corridors of Balmoral in your stretch-aerobic tights: 'I'm surprised you *noticed*', you say to your husband, who is off levitating with Indians.

You want to astonish the Comedy Store with a corrosive monologue about the Queen Mother's colostomy bag.

You'd settle for making jokes about Prince Charles's ears on Radio 4.

You end up writing for Jasper Carrott.

You want to bring in 100 cwt of coke on the tide, submerged beneath marker buoys.

You'd settle for posting an envelope of drugs to your widowed mother in Milton Keynes.

You end up in Uxbridge with a Customs Officer's fist up your arse.

You want to start a free glossy magazine for Knightsbridge and Chelsea to sell out for two million in five years.

You'd settle for selling out your free glossy magazine for £1,250 in five months, but keeping the Mercedes and share options for five years.

You end up being taken over by a sales agency and fired.

You want trial by jury.

You'd settle for trial by the media.

You end up in the back of a Transit van with six policemen jumping up and down on your spleen.

You want the office high-flyer to take you out of the typing pool and make you mistress of his heart.

You'd settle for a senior Vice President taking you to the Ritz in a limousine and making you mistress of his house.

You end up being taken to a wine bar by the Personnel Director who says, 'You be nice to me and I'll be nice to you.'

You want your publisher to say, '*Money* should have won the Booker Prize.'

You'd settle for your publisher saying, 'Martin Amis is the most interesting novelist in England.'

Your publisher says, 'It's such a shame Martin Amis has to write about such sordid people.'

You want your publisher to say, 'Astonishing! Overwhelming! You've invented a language for your characters.'

You'd settle for your publisher saying, 'A strange and impressive performance indeed!'

Your publisher says, 'In my opinion obscene language is a sign of a small vocabulary.'

You want to get into a prominent publishing house, discover a new metropolitan novelist and become his editor, inspiration and lover.

You'd settle for doing the picture research for *Great Walks of Britain*.

You end up typing out the publicity schedule for the author of *Please Miss You Can See The Angel's Bum*.

You want your publisher to phone.
You'd settle for your agent phoning.
Gibbens phones: 'Long time no see!'

FOUR

O lyric Love, half-angel and half-bird
And all a wonder and a wild desire

Robert Browning

You want to spend a romantic weekend in Manila with Mel Gibson.

You'd settle for a romantic weekend in Paris with Melvyn Bragg.

You end up in Glasgow with Mel Smith, and he brings a whippet into the bedroom and washes his smalls in the bidet. And you sleep in the bath – down the corridor.

You want to say, 'There is a magic about you, there is a glamour in your breasts and such promise in your mouth.'

You'd settle for saying, 'I imagine men are generally pretty intimidated by your father's money and your own obvious beauty.'

You hear yourself saying, 'Come on doll, you're gagging for it.'

You want to say, 'What about a burst of guilt-free recreational sex?'

You'd settle for saying, 'I'm only reliable for war-time romances, I'm afraid.'

You end up saying, 'Trust me. I mean it.'

You want him to compliment you on being as chic as a Parisienne.

You'd settle for him noticing your English rose complexion.

He looks at your calves and asks if you have German parents.

You want the French girl in the halter top who dances with you for half an hour and then goes off with Giscard.

You'd settle for Caroline who laughs at your jokes for half an hour and then goes off with Toby.

You end up with an Australian travel agent who sticks her tongue down your throat for half an hour and then says, 'I'm on at the moment but you can split me up the shitter if you want.'

You want him to say, 'Your body drives me wild; I must have you or I'll die.'

You'd settle for, 'What about it?'

You hear him saying, 'It's so nice being able to talk to a girl without the whole sex thing cropping up.'

You want him to grip you quickly.

You'd settle for him leaning across and kissing you firmly.

You end up with him leaning back and saying, 'Do you feel sexy or what?'

You want Charles Dance.

You'd settle for Jeremy Irons.

You get Lewis Collins.

He wants a girl in candy-striped jogging shorts.

He'd settle for a girl in designer jeans.

You've got a wardrobe full of ankle-length Indian print dresses.

You want him to say, 'You're the most beautiful girl I've ever met and life without you is agonising.'

You'd settle for him saying, 'You're so sexy it hurts, I'm in physical pain just looking at you.'

You hear him saying, 'What was the discipline like at your school?'

You imagine she's everything you want.

You believe she's everything you need.

You end up losing interest as soon as you know she'll do it, and her breath is heavy with red wine and sharp with nicotine.

You want to please your parents.

You settle for pleasing yourself.

You end up pleasing 85 Rude Boys who use your bed like a revolving door.

You want sex.

You'd settle for love.

You end up with a meaningful relationship.

You want her to lie there lost in physical rapture.

You'd settle for her being proudly, defiantly passive.

She ends up instructing you in a querulous, quacking voice, 'No, no, *slowly* – that *hurts,* Humphrey! Now *faster*! Don't stop! Remember what I like. That's better, slowly, but *firmly*. And touch my breasts. Gently! Don't *grab* them. *Stir* them. That's better. Now, harder, *harder,* bear down on me – and tell me how good it is for *you.*'

You want to take her gently while she sleeps.

You'd settle for her leaning into you with a drowsy smile, eyes closed.

She says, 'Is that you, Mark?'

You want to have multiple orgasms wracking your body and shaking the bed.

You'd settle for having an orgasm.

You end up faking an orgasm and telling him he's a wonderful lover.

You want an orgasm.

You'd settle for faking an orgasm.

You end up faking an erection.

You want her to say, 'You could kill me with that thing.'

You'd settle for 'WOW!'

She says, 'It looks like a penis only smaller.'

You want to carry his child.

You'd settle for carrying his luggage.

You end up carrying his drugs through Customs and doing six years in a Turkish jail.

You want a man whose love has an unwavering authority, setting things unchangeably in order.

You'd settle for a man who loves you.

You end up with a man who loves his mother.

You want Prince Philip.

You'd settle for Prince Charles.

You get Prince Andrew.

You want to be in *Tatler* enjoying a joke.

You'd settle for being in *Harpers & Queen* looking relaxed.

You end up in *Ritz* looking like a rat on a fishing line.

FIVE

How good is man's life,
The mere living!
how fit to employ
All the heart and the soul and the senses
Forever enjoy.

Robert Browning

You want to change the world.

You settle for changing your mind.

You end up changing your underwear.

You want a Bentley.

You'd settle for a Riley.

You've got a Volvo.

You want to sit in the sun and paint pictures.

You'd settle for laying out advertisements for a paint account.

You end up painting your house in the rain.

You want to raise £20 million to make a film.

You'd settle for raising £2 million to make a film.

You end up going to the cinema.

You want to develop a block of apartments.

You'd settle for pretending to develop a block of apartments.

You end up in a clinic.

You want to be a writer.

You'd settle for being a painter.

You end up in a clinic talking to the man pretending to be a property developer.

You want to stick to diet pills.

You'd settle for snorting coke.

You end up cooking coke, losing 4 stone in weight and being stretchered to the clinic where you talk to the man pretending to be the writer who's talking to the man pretending to be the property developer.

You want to put half your capital into Australian mining shares and retire to a Georgian country house with a girl whose father's an Earl.

You'd settle for putting a quarter for your capital into oil futures and retiring to the Home Counties with a stockbroker's daughter.

You end up losing three months' salary at a roulette table and bouncing a cheque on your father-in-law.

You want to be hard but fair and fire your friends.

You'd settle for being cruel but kind and firing your employees.

You end up stern but stupid and getting fired.

You want to go up to that yob in the train who's punching his wife in the face and take him apart.

You'd settle for saying, 'Would you care to come and sit with me, my dear?'

You end up stepping in feebly with the words, 'Excuse me –', and getting a flat hand across your face while all the commuters hide their embarrassment.

You want to win the Booker Prize with a metropolitan novel written on a strange frequency.

You'd settle for making £60,000 a year writing Christmas toilet books called *Up The Cistern* by Jimmy Riddle.

You end up as the Entertainments Editor for the *Mail on Sunday*.

You want to go poolside in L.A. and write screenplays for Michael Cimino.

You'd settle for a boxy office at Warner's rewriting Michael Cimino's rewrites.

You end up in the L.A. hills writing treatments for a mini-series featuring Robert Culp and Tuesday Weld.

You want to get into directing.

You'd settle for getting into showbusiness.

You end up getting into the management team of a theme restaurant in Leicester Square.

You want to say, 'Your overdraft charges are iniquitous, but if I'm prepared to live with them I don't see why you shouldn't be.'

You'd settle for saying, 'It's my overdraft and I'll do what I want with it.'

You end up saying, 'Look sir, about my overdraft. My girlfriend's in a lot of trouble with drugs, and I'm *pretty* certain she'll end up in prison, which, of course, will make her story very valuable. Here's a photograph of her – she's dancing on a table in Ibiza. Anyway, it's an extraordinary story with all the right ingredients – orgies, violence, police corruption, drugs. Have you ever freebased? The point is, I'm absolutely certain I can interest a publisher in it. The serial rights to the *News of the World* alone must be worth £20,000. Have you read *In Cold Blood* by Truman Capote? Well, it would be like that, but . . . *colder* – as long as she *does* go to prison of course . . .'

You want to say, 'Out of my way, you sordid old cow!' You're drunk! Your hair's a mess, you haven't washed – the state you're in! Good grief!'

You'd settle for saying, 'Actually, there's a queue here and I rather think I was in front of you.'

You end up saying, 'No, no, please, you go ahead.'

You want to be liberated, enjoy nights out with the girls and only see him twice a week.

You'd settle for not having to stay in every night waiting for him to ring.

You hear yourself offering to wash his shirts if he'll come round at weekends.

When the estate agent says, 'Excuse the coons two doors down,' you want to say, 'You ugly racist, I'm off.'

You'd settle for saying, 'As a matter of fact my mother's a Negress.'

You end up saying, 'Perhaps I could offer a couple of grand less on the house, then?'

You want to have a washboard stomach and a black belt in Eastern fighting systems.

You'd settle for demoralising yobs in shopping malls with educated sarcasms and an acid gentlemanliness.

You end up handing your girlfriend to a 13-year-old Chelsea supporter before he shows you his knife.

You want to be the nippy little winger getting to the byline and crossing the ball to the big silly lad in the No. 9 shirt.

You'd settle for being an unhurried mid-field general with bags of skill on the ball and an educated left foot, sending beautifully weighted passes to the big silly lad in the No. 9 shirt.

You end up as the big silly lad in the No. 9 shirt.

You wanted to be Bobby Charlton.

You'd have settled for being Jack Charlton.

You end up playing social football on wet Wednesdays against a team of 55-year-old porcelain experts from the Victoria and Albert Museum and their striker scores five goals with his artificial leg.

You want to be respected as the heavy centre of a metropolitan circle.

You'd settle for being a pub bore.

You end up putting a humorous announcement on your answering machine.

You want to insult Roger Scruton at a dinner party.

You'd settle for cancelling your subscription to *The Salisbury Review*.

You end up sitting next to black people on buses to show you like them.

You want to care about other people and vote Labour.

You'd settle for looking as though you care about other people and voting SDP.

You end up caring about yourself and voting Tory. 'I've tried voting Tory from time to time and I can handle it. I'm out of work, and my father's out of work, and my mother's waiting to go into hospital, and my sister's on the game, and the electricity's been cut off, and my brother's been killed in the Falklands, and we haven't any money, but I can handle it. And there's always heroin.'

You want to be a good conversationalist.

You'd settle for being a good listener.

You end up telling every dinner table you sit at: 'Do you know, I was the first boy at my school who knew how "schism" was pronounced?"

You want a glass of white wine before dinner and bed by eleven.

You'd settle for half a bottle of scotch and bed by one.

You end up shitfaced in the Fulham Road at 5 a.m., and you've forgotten where you've parked the car and you've lost your shoe.

You want a cheque in the post.

You'd settle for a bill in the post.

You get a letter from Customs and Excise setting up a date for a VAT inspection.

You want a love letter.

You'd settle for an invitation to a pyjama party.

You end up with a letter from a V.D. clinic as your name's been given, but they don't say by whom.

You want to open a bookshop-cum-coffee house in Bloomsbury where intellectuals can meet and exchange ideas.

You'd settle for a second-hand bookstall at Camden Lock.

You end up with a Kwik-Print franchise in Hammersmith.

You want to be paid in cash.

You'd settle for being paid in 90 days.

You get a letter from the receiver saying the company's gone bust with £400 left in the kitty and you're 42nd on the list.

SIX

There's nothing nobler nor more admirable than when two people who see eye to eye keep house as man and wife confounding their enemies and delighting their friends.

Homer

You want to be married in 120 yards of tulle at the Holy Trinity Brompton.

You'd settle for being married in a marquee overlooking your father's lake.

You end up being married in Chelsea Registry Office and you're five months pregnant.

You wanted to marry the boy next door.

You settled for marrying a pop star.

You end up with a woman's magazine asking you every ten years how you reassembled your life in Warrington after your husband traded you in for a movie star.

You wanted to marry a blonde actress.

You settled for marrying a sturdy Sloane.

You end up drinking Spanish champagne and telling nightclub hostesses you love them.

You wanted to marry a man who works for Watneys and should have married a sturdy Sloane.

You settled for marrying a man who puts on musicals and should have married a blonde actress.

You end up as a cleaner in a psychiatric hospital.

You wanted to marry a man who puts on musicals and who should have married a blonde actress.

You settled for a man who works for Watneys and should have married a sturdy girl.

You ended up with six children who won't speak to you even at Christmas.

You want to be a mannequin.

You settled for being a model.

You end up in the 'Readers' Wives' section of *Knave*.

You want two little boys in knickerbockers with beautiful manners.

You'd settle for two little boys who got into Oxford.

You end up with two little boys who scream when they don't get a present, who bite smaller children, who lie freely, who have tantrums in Safeways, who throw ashtrays at their psychiatrists, whose chins are covered in mucous and who get arrested for shoplifting at the age of eight.

You want to buy the house from which you'll never have to move, a house to recapture the summers of your youth, the long days and apple blossom, the sound of girls playing tennis in the softening light, a house with room for three children and a nanny, with a 5-acre garden and a willow tree and a paddock for a pony.

You settle for offering 20 per cent under the asking price for two derelict houses in the wrong part of Chiswick which will take three years to rebuild.

Your wife makes you withdraw the offer before the owners have time to reject it and you lose your deposit, though you're not sure why.

You want a marital relationship akin to that of two planets revolving around each other – mutually dependant, but separate.

You'd settle for a painful exploration of each other's strengths and weaknesses.

You end up at it like knives in the back of a Ford Granada with someone else's wife.

You want a marriage and a career.

You'd settle for one or the other.

You end up sinking into your grievances with a vain ignorant man who values your matrimonial contribution at £2 an hour.

You want to say, 'Help! No one likes me, I'm so fat and I haven't any friends.'

You'd settle for saying, 'Do you think I'm too fat? Is that why you never touch me any more?'

You end up saying, 'You're getting so fat. I suppose it's my fault, is it? Everything's *my* fault.'

You want him to congratulate you on your *crème brûlée*.

You'd settle for him eating it with obvious pleasure.

He says, 'Am I supposed to eat this burnt bit?' and suppresses a belch.

You want him to compliment you on your figure-hugging dress and scarlet lipstick.

You'd settle for him noticing that you've changed out of your dungarees.

He says, 'Do you really want to come to the party, sausage? There's an awfully good film on the box.'

You want an intelligent man.

You'd settle for a man who made you laugh.

You end up with a man who wears a yellow pullover and says, 'Don't tell me!'

You want Max Beerbohm.

You'd settle for Max Miller.

You end up with Max Hastings.

You want to impress your mother-in-law's dinner party with your wit and penetrating intelligence.

You'd settle for saying something superior but not condescending every 20 minutes.

After two hours silence you hear yourself saying, 'You have to be careful how you write "Clint", otherwise it looks like "Clunt".

You want her to astonish the table with five insights into famine relief.

You'd settle for her saying something original about Bob Geldof's moral position.

You hear her saying, 'Do you think I'm too fat?'

You want him to be protective and gallant.

You'd settle for him letting you speak.

He groans and says, 'Oh God! She opens her mouth and out it comes!'

You want her to be impressed by your National Service experience in submarines.

You'd settle for her not falling asleep.

She says, '1953? Heavens! I was only four!'

You want her to say, 'Isn't she gorgeous!'

You'd settle for her saying nothing.

She says, '*I* wouldn't pose for *Penthouse* if they paid me a thousand pounds.'

You want to love, honour and obey.

You settle for obeying because you haven't any money.

You end up living in Wolverhampton saying, 'I don't mind what he does as long as I don't know about it.'

You want to ignore what he does as long as you don't know about it.

You'd settle for going through his pockets.

You end up breaking into his filing cabinet and finding a video of him performing with your best friend.

You want to say nothing to your second best girlfriend.

You'd settle for saying, 'And how's your attractive husband?'

You end up saying, 'Better you hear it from me than from someone who doesn't like you.'

You want an open marriage.

You'd settle for an understanding marriage.

You end up playing the key game in Croydon with electricians and their wives.

You want to say nothing.

You'd settle for saying, 'Did you have a nice time?'

You end up saying, 'Did you like him? Did you find him attractive? How attractive exactly? Did he try and kiss you? Did you *want* him to kiss you? What were you doing in the car for so long? What were you talking about? Are you telling me that you were together for three hours and he didn't try to touch you? Did he say anything about me?'

You want him to say nothing.

You'd settle for him denying it.

He ends up admitting it.

You want him to admit it.

You'd settle for him denying it.

He ends up boasting about it.

You want an extra-curricular mistress because your wife shops and cooks and wears red washing-up gloves and pantyhose, and she's fat and disappointed and she eats apples in bed forming an echo-chamber in her mouth, and she sits around in a face-pack and says, 'I'm worried about our relationship', and she won't let you watch the snooker on the television because it clashes with *EastEnders,* and she says, 'I like oysters but they don't like me,' and 'Ours not to reason why.' You will spend three nights a week with your mistress in her penthouse overlooking Chelsea Bridge, where she will lie on a *chaise longue* in her underwear looking at her wardrobe of customised clothing.

You settle for moving your mistress into a one-room flat off the Munster Road because she once danced for you in a yellow G-string.

You end up living with your mistress in her one-room flat off the Munster Road, and she shops and cooks and wears green washing-up gloves, and she eats crisps in bed and puts on 12 lb and she won't let you watch the snooker on the television because it clashes with *Crossroads* and she says, 'If you can't be good be careful!' and 'Pardon my French!' and you miss your wife and your haemorrhoids explode.

You want her to say, 'I've met someone else.'

You'd settle for her saying, 'You don't own me, you know, I'm free to go.'

She says, 'Hold me. I'm so frightened.'

You want to say, 'You're driving me mad.'

You'd settle for saying, 'Let's have a trial separation.'

You end up saying, 'Don't be frightened. I'll look after you. I love you.'

Richard Ingrams

(See page 96)

You want

You'd settle for

You end up with

You wanted to be a rugby referee.

You'd have settled for being a rich businessman.

You end up as an extra at the Tory party Conferen beaming like a farmer whose pig has won first prize

You want to be Mandy Rice-Davies.

You'd settle for being Sarah Keays.

You end up as Ann Parkinson.

You want to punch
Dirk Bogarde.

You'd settle for punching
Kenneth Williams.

You end up punching
Peter Cook, thinking he's
Kenneth Williams.

You want to behave with dignity when she leaves you.

You'd settle for listening to the words of Country and Western songs and walking alone in graveyards.

You end up wearing a topcoat over Chinese pyjamas to do the shopping in Europa stores and sleeping in a telephone box under her window, clutching a sheaf of her letters.

You want to behave with dignity when he leaves you.

You'd settle for crying on your own in the dark.

You end up washing his mistress's knickers because her washing machine has broken down.

When he comes back you want him to say, 'I must have been mad. It's you I love. The sex was a nightmare.'

You'd settle for him saying, 'I must have been mad. I've hurt you dreadfully. Will you ever forgive me?'

He says, 'I must have been mad. I'm so comfortable here. It's like putting on a pair of old slippers. The cats look well.'

When she comes back you want her to say, 'My God how I missed you! I could never have imagined how much I'd miss you.'

You'd settle for her saying, 'Yes it was good, but not as good as this.'

She says, 'I hope you're not going to lecture me.'

You want an amicable divorce.

You'd settle for a civilised divorce.

You end up arguing over the wall-lights while the children cry on the landing.

SEVEN

You want to be 25.
You'd settle for being 35.
You're 45.

You want to fly fighter jets.

You'd settle for flying passenger jets.

You end up flying back from Brussels, business class.

You want to be British.

You'd settle for being Canadian.

You're Australian.

You want to say, 'You've given up sex? Get into those stirrups!'

You'd settle for saying, 'You've given up sex? What's the point of you then?'

You hear yourself saying, 'Yes, women have certainly earned the right to take responsibility for their own bodies.'

You want to write like Martin Amis.

You'd settle for quoting his jokes to your friends.

You end up plagiarising him for a toilet book.

You want to say, 'Madam, I am merely drunk. But you are ugly, and I shall be sober in the morning.'

You'd settle for saying, 'Drunk, yes, but happy, and how many of us can say that, Bessie?'

You end up saying, 'Maybe I am drunk, but at least *my* husband isn't fucking his tax advisor!'

You want to say, 'Good gracious you're ugly!'

You'd settle for saying, 'What are you bimbos trying to prove going round in boiler suits?'

You hear yourself saying, 'I don't deny there were anomalies to be ironed out, but does Libby Purves *have* to breastfeed her babies at parties?'

You want to say, 'You must be mad!'

You'd settle for saying, 'I'm afraid . . . I've got a headache.'

You hear yourself saying, 'Great, yes, of course.'

You want her to say, 'It's getting late and I've got a breakfast meeting. I'll call you a cab.'

You'd settle for her falling asleep so you can call yourself a cab.

She peels off her panto stocking and says, 'If I open another bottle of plonk shall we hit the sack, or what?'

She wants to say, 'Go to bed with you? You must be mad! You're fat and bald, you've got hairy wrists and a medallion. I'm sorry but you're revolting!'

She'd settle for saying, 'Go to bed with you? You must be mad! You're fat and bald. I'm sorry but you're revolting!'

She says, 'Go to bed with you? You must be mad. You're revolting.'

You want to be a barrister.

You'd settle for being a solicitor.

You end up as a lay magistrate lecturing barristers and solicitors who can't answer back because you're a magistrate.

You want to be schoolmasters.

You'd settle for writing school musicals.

You end up as Tim Rice and Andrew Lloyd Webber.

You want an offer from Australia, packaged as a pool, a Porsche and the deeds to a small European principality.

You'd settle for a Vice Presidency in a provincial agency.

You end up weeping at your London Chairman and begging for a last chance at a lower salary.

You want to join the SAS, sitting in puddles and coming through windows on wrecking balls.

You'd settle for a larger penis and smaller feet.

You end up editing the *Daily Telegraph*.

You want love.

You'd settle for sex.

You end up abusing yourself in a bedsit off the Munster Road, and you haven't had a bath for a week.

You wanted to be a Casanova.

You'd have settled for being a comedian.

You end up as Peter Cook.

You wanted to be Head Prefect.

You'd have settled for not sleeping on rubber sheets.

You end up as a member of the National Viewers and Listeners Association.

You wanted to be Sir Winston Churchill.

You'd settle for being Randolph Churchill.

You end up as Winston Churchill, MP.

You wanted to be the grand old man of Japanese literature.

You'd have settled for preserving the racial and moral purity of the nation with a cadre of firm young men in military shorts.

You end up committing hara-kiri on TV while a disciple swipes off your head with an 18th-century sword.

You want to be a Death Wish vigilante shooting rapists with a very big handgun.

You'd settle for saving a girl from jeering football fans.

You end up punching your wife and making her nose bleed.

You want everyone to be frightened of you.

You'd settle for everyone liking you.

You end up as Nigel Dempster.

You want everyone to like you.

You'd settle for everyone being frightened of you.

You end up as Peter McKay.

You wanted to be able to write.

You'd have settled for being able to read.

You end up editing 'Pseud's Corner'.

You want to be 'provocative'.

You'd settle for being 'never less than stimulating'.

You end up being silly and writing for the *Sunday Telegraph*. 'I wish I could believe that the long-term Broadmoore prisoner would be *less* of a danger to the general public rather than more as a result of his studying sociology at the Open University.'

You wanted to be respected.

You settle for being celebrated.

You end up on 'Pro/Celebrity Knockout' sliding down a chute into a vat of slime.

You wanted to be Russell Davies.

You'd have settled for being Russell Harty.

You end up as Russell Grant.

You wanted to lecture the International Monetary Fund.

You'd have settled for lecturing your wife on her housekeeping budget.

You end up querying your bank charges and saving £2.43.

You want to direct films.

You'd settle for directing an episode of 'Minder'.

You end up at the Coach and Horses talking about your last commercial and trying to raise Verity Lambert on the pay-phone, but it's too late at night, you're too drunk, there's a queue for the lavatory, Jeffrey Bernard has been sick over your shoes, and your fat wife is waiting for you in Maidenhead with an increasingly frightened expression on her face.

You want to be Michael Cimino.

You'd settle for being Michael Douglas.

You end up as Michael Winner.

You want Clint Eastwood and Sondra Locke.
You'd settle for Charles Bronson and Jill Ireland.
You get Robert Wagner and Stephanie Powers.

You want Randolph Scott.
You'd settle for Howard Duff.
You get Ronald Reagan.

You want Al Pacino.
Forget it.

You want Walter Matthau.
You'd settle for Ernest Borgnine.
You get Jack Klugman.

You want Robert Redford and Goldie Hawn.
You'd settle for George Segal and Glenda Jackson.
You get Roger Moore and Susannah York.

You want Sam Neil and Rachel Ward.
You'd settle for Charles Dance and Diana Quick.
You get John Nettles and Liza Goddard.

You want Bob Hoskins.

You'd settle for Lewis Collins.

You get Patrick Mower.

You wanted to be a comic actress and a good sport.

You'd have settled for being compassionate and appearing in televised snowball fights with spastics.

You end up as Maureen Lipman talking patronisingly about her mother to Bel Mooney and wearing a chamber pot for the cover of a toilet book.

You want to produce plays and sleep with actresses.

You'd settle for backing plays and seeing actresses in their underwear.

You end up in Bournemouth in a false nose and dark glasses hiding from your accountant behind an answerphone.

You want to see Natasha Redgrave in her underwear.

You'd settle for seeing Corin Redgrave in his underwear.

You end up seeing Vanessa Redgrave in her underwear.

You want to be Michael Codron.

You'd settle for being Michael White.

You end up as Cameron Mackintosh.

You want Paul Schofield and Vanessa Redgrave.

You'd settle for Donald Sinden and Diana Rigg.

You get Paul Daneman and Nanette Newman.

You want Albert Finney.
You'd settle for Nicol Williamson.
You get Peter O'Toole.

You want Prunella Scales.
You'd settle for Julie Walters.
You get Barbara Windsor.

You want Alison Steadman.
You'd settle for Julie Walters.
You get Maureen Lipman.

You want Robert Robinson to host 'Points of View'.
You'd settle for Clive James hosting 'Points of View'.
Barry Took hosts 'Points of View'.

You want to host a chat show.

You'd settle for being amusing on a chat show.

You end up talking about codpieces on 'Wogan'.

You want Jonathan Miller to appear on your chat show.

You'd settle for Peter Ustinov.

You get Leslie Thomas.

You want Jonathan Miller.

You'd settle for Desmond Morris.

You get James Burke.

You want Alan Coren.

You'd settle for Robert Morley.

You get Arthur Marshall.

You want to be on 'Question Time'.

You'd settle for being on 'Start The Week'.

You end up on 'The Joan Rivers Show' being upstaged by a frog.

You want Alan Bennet.

You'd settle for John Mortimer.

You end up with Ray Connolly writing for Peter Bowles. 'And what brings *you* to the – er – Street of *Shame*!?!'

You want to ignore the critics.

You'd settle for pretending to ignore the critics.

You end up writing to the *Spectator*, 'Dear sir, my attention has been drawn to Christopher Booker's all too generous review of my book, *The Mathematics of Steady State Theory*. However . . .'

You want to be a man of letters like Rupert Hart-Davis.

You'd settle for being an educated vicar.

You end up as John Julius Norwich.

You want to be a man of letters like John Julius Norwich.

You'd settle for using the word 'disagreeable' sixteen times in one *Spectator* essay.

You end up as Geoffrey Wheatcroft.

You want a Foreword by Prince Charles.

You'd settle for one by Prince Philip.

You get one by Princess Michael of Kent.

You want to be an expert on Flaubert.

You'd settle for writing a *Dictionary of Received Ideas*.

You end up saying, 'Irony's a two-edged sword.'

You want to say to your publisher, 'It's a tribute to Flaubert, you turkey.'

You'd settle for saying, 'Well, it's loosely based on an idea of Flaubert's, do you see?'

You hear yourself saying, 'Not that I'm comparing myself to Julian Barnes, of course.'

You want to write like Julian Barnes.

You'd settle for having your novels reviewed by the *Sunday Telegraph*.

You end up writing like A. N. Wilson.

You want to call Lord Hailsham a slippery old buffoon.

You'd settle for calling Leon Brittan a balloon-faced toad.

You end up calling Charlotte Cornwall a floppy-bottomed actress and paying $10,000 in libel damages plus costs.

You want Louis Basualdo, Chevy Chase, Enzo Apicella, Tom Stoppard, Christopher Reeve, Tula, Princess Alexandra Galitzine, Ronald Dworkin, Mikhail Baryshnikov, Miranda Guinness, Prince Stash Klossowski, Lord Lucan and Martin Amis to come to your party.

You'd settle for Lady Rothermere, Lord Weidenfeld, Michael White, Amanda Lear, Nigel Pollitzer, Lady Melchett, Clive James, Miriam Stoppard, Rudolf Nureyev, Sabrina Guinness and Kingsley Amis coming to your party.

Liz Brewer, Jeremy Beadle, Lionel Blair, Lionel Bart, Paul Raymonde, Alexander Walker, Molly Parkin, Taki, Ricci Burns, Cleo Rocas, Karen Stringfellow, Pat Booth, Nigel Oaks, Dave Lee-Travis, Jeremy Brown, Tony Hickox, Mynah Bird, Gilbert Lloyd, April Ashley, Viviane Ventura, Jonathan King, Craig Mackenzie, Lindy Benson, Nigel Dempster, Richard Compton Miller, Wayne Sleep, Peter Cook, Paula Yates, Ian Botham, Oliver Reed, Viscount Althorp, David Lichfield, Vickie Hodge, Gyles Brandreth, Patrick Mower, Samantha Fox, Samantha Fox's mother, Richard Stilgoe, Bill Oddie, Angie Best, Mark Thatcher, Larry Adler, Gloria Hunniford, Jeffrey Archer, Janet Street-Porter, Margaret, Duchess of Argyll, Jack Tinker, Russell Grant, Robert Carrier, Victor Kiam, Jamie Blandford, Daphne Guinness, Suzanne Daniel, Buster Mottram and John Amis come to your party.

You want to say, 'Oh Christ, I'll obviously have to get drunk.'

You'd settle for saying, 'Listening to housewives quoting from the *Daily Mail* is so draining.'

You hear yourself saying, 'If only Lord Longford would show a little *less* concern for the criminal, and a little *more* for the victim of his crime.'

You want to talk to Julie Burchill.

You'd settle for talking to Katherine Whitehorn.

You end up talking to Lynda Lee-Potter.

You want to say, 'If you don't stop talking ignorant nonsense about Pamela Stephenson I'll pull your nose.'

You'd settle for saying, 'Pamela Stephenson's originality consisted of the fact that she was a pretty girl telling dirty jokes – unfortunately she never seemed to understand her material, even when it was funny.'

You hear yourself saying, 'You didn't shock us, Pam, love, you merely bored us.'

You want to say, 'Actually, the Queen Mother's a merciless old pro and, far from being the perfect granny, she doesn't even like children.'

You'd settle for saying, 'I suppose the years must take their toll, but she is only 86 after all.'

You hear youself saying, 'I deplore cowardly attacks on people in the public eye who can't answer back.'

You want to say, 'Mike Yarwood's a soft and ingratiating wimp.'

You'd settle for saying, 'No wonder he was Harold Wilson's favourite impersonator.'

You end up saying, 'The best satirists always respect their targets.'

You want to say, 'You're the stupidest man I've ever met at a party. Push off.'

You'd settle for saying, 'No doubt he took a year to write *The Merry Wives of Windsor,* but finished *Lear* in a weekend.'

You hear yourself saying, 'You're right, of course. Wasn't it that wise and agreeable man John Mortimer who pointed out that any fool can write a tragedy, but that writing a comedy requires real skill?'

You want to talk to John Gross.

You'd settle for talking to Miriam Gross.

You end up talking to Geoffrey Wheatcroft.

You wanted to be radical.

You settled for being the middle-brow's highbrow.

You end up writing *Yet Another Voyage Round My Father*.

You want to avoid Peter Cook at a party, so frightened are you of saying something wrong.

You'd settle for smiling vaguely at him across the room.

You end up buttonholing him, 'Of course the only reason Dudley Moore's so successful is that he's attractive to women and you're not.'

You want to say, 'If you tell another joke I'll cry.'

You'd settle for saying, 'I like that joke. I've always liked that joke.'

You end up saying, 'Ha ha, that's one to remember, I'll have to make a note of that one!'

You want to be Rik Mayall.

You'd settle for being Ben Elton.

You end up picking your nose on camera for no discernible reason.

You want to say, 'You horse! He's a careerist, a climber, a *personality*. All that talent he's spent on making himself *popular*!'

You'd settle for saying, 'I'm not sure whether he's made a joke since 1979.'

You end up saying, 'Yes, of course, Clive James is a brilliantly amusing man, but we British love to knock our heroes.'

You want to be a rake.

You'd settle for being raffish.

You end up saying, 'In the good old days when Soho was Bohemian rather than sordid . . .'

You want to be thought a hard man.

You'd settle for being thought a shit.

You end up being called a turd.

You want a torso like Rambo pulsating with rippling muscle.

You'd settle for a slight bulge in the biceps.

You catch your nose in your bullworker and can't show yourself for a week.

You want to be a film star.

You'd settle for being 'pretty girl at party' in an episode of 'The Professionals'.

You end up on the game, showing your old portfolio to Arabs.

You want him to say, 'I can only stay for half an hour, here's £50.'

You'd settle for him saying, 'I can only stay for an hour, here's £100.'

He says, 'I really want to get to know you as a person.'

You want to be a pimp.

You'd settle for being a ponce.

You end up as a punter, tied to a whipping stool by a bewildered girl who once appeared in an episode of 'The Professionals'.

You want to commit the perfect crime, stealing £10 million from an organisation that won't miss it.

You'd settle for embezzling half a million from your East End employers.

You end up as a one-legged shoplifter pilfering the shoe racks outside Dolcis.

You want to kidnap Richard Ingrams and photograph him with two nude schoolboys.

You'd settle for insulting him in a Christmas toilet book.

You end up weeping with gratitude when he nods at you in Greek Street.

You want to say, 'Stuff my career! And my wife! And my three dumpy daughters! I'm only 50 and I want to be happy!'

You'd settle for saying, 'They're welcome to the house and half my money. They're better off without me.'

You end up trying to rebuild your career and doing community work in the East End and being photographed with your wife outside the village church on Sunday.

You want to say, 'My Lord, I regret to have to tell you that I am profoundly guilty and can only place myself at the mercy of the court.'

You'd settle for saying, 'I'm so sorry. I can't speak. That's all I have to say.'

You end up saying, 'It wasn't my fault, I was told to, they made me, they said they'd kill me, I didn't have any money, I'd lost my shoe, my friends are all dying and I haven't had a holiday since 1976.'

You want your daughter to marry a Lord.

You'd settle for your daughter working for Quartet Books.

You end up with a daughter who takes drugs and burns the house down.

You want Miranda Guinness.

You'd settle for Sabrina Guinness.

You end up with Daphne Guinness.

You want freedom for you both.

You'd settle for freedom for yourself.

You end up looking painfully at the glow in your wife's eyes when she looks at younger men.

You want to take a villa in the south of France and fill it with oiled actresses and women of Hungarian birth.

You'd settle for taking a villa on a Greek island and filling it with girls who live in bedsits and go to bottle parties.

You end up advertising in *Private Eye* as a 'Non-smoking executive looking for a lively divorcee to share his assets in Ibiza.'

You want to move out to a penthouse to wallow in a trench of sex.

You'd settle for sending your wife on holiday by herself so you can fill up the flat with agency girls.

You end up stuck in a holiday let at £400 a week going through your telephone book. You can't work, you can't think, you're tired of watching *The Streets of San Francisco* on your own, the bed's unmade, the light in the kitchen's too bright, the wallpaper's unfamiliar, the unread Sunday supplements are piling up, the fridge is empty, you miss the cats, you're very cold and it will soon be Christmas. You catch sight of yourself in a shop window and you're going bald.

You want Lucy to phone.

You'd settle for Tracey phoning.

Gibbens phones, 'Hullo stranger! How about lunch?'

You want to sleep with Lucy.

You'd settle for taking Lucy to lunch.

You end up providing an alibi for Lucy so she can sleep with Gibbens.

You want to go back to Sicily to the hotel where you had your honeymoon, and leave the children with mother.

You'd settle for a week on the Norfolk Broads leaving the children at school.

You end up with the children at Broadstairs while he plays golf in the Algarve.

You want to take him for everything he's got.

You'd settle for taking the house and half the money.

You end up boastfully standing by him in the blaze of unaccustomed publicity.

EIGHT

Is it so small a thing
To have enjoyed the sun
To have lived late in the Spring
to have loved, to have thought, to have done.

Matthew Arnold

You want the girl and the money at 25.

You'd settle for the girl and the money at 35.

You end up with the girl and the money at 55 and it's too late and your legs have turned blue.

You want to be The Voice of Reason.

You'd settle for being The Man They Can't Gag.

You end up as Claude Duval the Punter's Pal.

You want to be clever.

You'd settle for being stupid.

You end up as Sir David English.

You want to be clever but wise.

You'd settle for being small but grave.

You end up as Bernard Levin writing like an elephant with a wet mouth, 'Why had I walked from the Camargue to the High Alps? What I sought might have been behind any hedge I walked past . . . and perhaps beyond that there is peace and serenity and understanding, even the answer to the very last question of all – since we must die, why must we live first?'

You want to be a Tory backbencher.

You'd settle for inflaming suburban paranoia by waving a pair of handcuffs above your head at the Tory Party Conference.

You end up exposing yourself to minors and getting off on the grounds of insufficient evidence.

You wanted to be Governor of Holloway.

You'd have settled for being Richard Ingrams.

You end up as Mary Whitehouse.

You wanted to be a Brigadier.

You'd settle for being a Lieutenant-Colonel.

You end up as a remaindered Major, looking for a job as a gardener.

You want to write a serious novel.

You'd settle for writing an educated thriller.

You end up as a tax exile in Ireland wandering around a 50-acre estate, and you haven't any friends, and a pigeon has just shat in your eye and your arrangements with the Revenue keep you in Ireland for another three years.

You wanted to be a sensitive actor.

You'd have settled for being a sensitive novelist.

You end up as Dirk Bogarde writing *Flower Arranging Was For Sundays*.

You wanted to be Edith Evans.

You'd have settled for being Dora Bryan.

You end up as Kenneth Williams.

You want to be Lord Beaverbrook.

You'd settle for being Rupert Murdoch.

You end up as Robert Maxwell.

You want to be a smart arse.

You'd settle for being a silly arse.

You end up as an arsehole.

You wanted to be Michael Caine.

You'd have settled for being Nigel Davenport talking on television about 'my great chum Mike Caine' in a peculiar deep voice.

You end up in a boarding house with a trouser-press and one suit for detergent auditions, teaching English as a foreign language.

You wanted to be Lawrence of Arabia.

You'd have settled for anything.

You end up as Michael Heseltine.

You wanted to be Prime Minister.

You'd have settled for resigning from the Cabinet in a blaze of publicity.

You end up as a stooped derelict on the back benches with your head coming out of your chest.

You wanted to be a serious politician.

You'd have settled for being a personality politician.

You end up on 'Question Time' agreeing with Paul Johnson.

You wanted to be a serious historian.

You'd have settled for being a popular historian.

You end up as Paul Johnson fantasising that the Queen has summoned you to Balmoral where she invites you to form an alternative government of people who live in the real world.

You wanted to be a serious writer.

You'd have settled for being a serious politician.

You end up writing facetious end-pieces and hand-jiving sheepishly with Mrs Hattersley at the Notting Hill Carnival.

You wanted to be Boadicea.

You'd have settled for being General de Gaulle.

You end up with mad eyes and a wet top lip making a party political broadcast from Colonel H's grave.

You wanted to wear a headscarf and carry a Georgian soup tureen through a field of little feathered corpses and a sheet of Highland rain.

You'd have settled for being a disappointed housewife with four ungrateful children.

You end up having to dance with black politicians, afraid to abdicate in case Raine Spencer becomes Queen Mother.

You wanted to be eccentric.

You'd settle for being a character.

You end up an hour late for everything wearing odd socks.

You wanted to play cricket for England.

You'd have settled for playing cricket for the Old Salopians with your trousers held up by an I Zingari tie.

You end up queueing with your son for Richie Benaud's autograph among the plastic lager cups and vomiting Australians.

You wanted to be Eddie Villella.

You'd have settled for being John Travolta.

You end up doing the Gay Gordons with your arse sticking out at the Midland Bank Staff Ball.

You wanted to be a surgeon.

You'd settle for being a society osteopath.

You end up as a damp palmed psychic claiming to alter destiny by manipulation of the sexual organs.

You want to be a psychiatrist.

You'd settle for being a psychologist.

You end up as an agony aunt dishing out uneducated catchphrases on Capital Radio.

You want to be a young fogey.

You'd settle for being an old fogey.

You end up an old fart.

You want to be Charles Moore.

You'd settle for being Alexander Chancellor.

You end up as Richard West.

You want to see your name in the papers.

You'd settle for being the corpse at a funeral.

You end up as Malcolm Muggeridge.

You wanted to be rational.

You'd have settled for being reasonable.

You end up as an atheist reading your stars in the *Daily Mail*.

You want to be rational.

You'd settle for being reasonable.

You end up saying, 'I don't believe in organised religion, but if I were involved in a plane crash I think I'd say my prayers.'

You want to be a nurse.

You settle for being a social worker.

You end up spying on unmarried mothers to see if their boyfriends are living in.

You want to be a campaigning journalist exposing pharmaceutical gene-damage.

You'd settle for being a consumer watchdog exposing bucketshop brokers.

You end up on the *News of the World*, exposing wife-swapping school teachers who then commit suicide.

You want to be a serious journalist.

You'd settle for reviewing books for the *Daily Mail*.

You end up saying, 'Say what you will, Sir David English is the complete professional.'

You want to be Graham Garden.

You'd settle for being Tim Brooke-Taylor.

You end up as Bill Oddie.

You want to be witty.

You'd settle for being facetious.

You end up introducing 'Film '86' with a string of impudent banalities.

You want to be funny.

You'd settle for finding other people funny.

You end up saying, 'Thank goodness I'm one of those extraordinary people who can laugh at themselves.'

You want to say, 'I remember when the twins were born, I went to bed that night and had a long and troubled sleep, and when I woke up I was 50.'

You'd settle for saying, 'Is this all there is? Sitting at opposite ends of the sofa watching the World Figure Skating Championships from Geneva.'

You end up saying, 'This is cosy.'

You want to mature as you grow.

You'd settle for acquiring acquired tastes.

You end up caring more about what you eat than who you sleep with.

You want to grow old gracefully.

You'd settle for growing old tactfully.

You end up tap dancing at your daughter's wedding with your dress caught in your hair.

You want to be the Duchess of Kent.

You'd settle for being the Duchess of Devonshire.

You end up the Duchess of Argyll.

You want to grow old gracefully.

You'd settle for growing old tactfully.

You end up representing Greece in the world Karate Championship at the age of fifty and as you enter the ring your liver bursts and your nose drops off.

You wanted to be laughably rich.

You'd have settled for being seriously rich.

You end up as a paranoid in a hotel suite, surrounded by burly men and smart lawyers, too afraid to go out in case you're sued by chorus girls.

You wanted to travel light and see the world.

You'd have settled for travelling up the Amazon with a tent and a Bunsen burner.

You end up travelling round and round the Circle Line with all your possessions in a paper bag.

You wanted a Georgian house in Somerset with five acres and a wood.

You'd have settled for a wing in a subdivided Victorian mansion with access to joint gardens.

You end up in a mock-Tudor semi in Guildford with clock golf and padda tennis.

You wanted to work for yourself.

You'd have settled for working for your father.

You end up working for your son.

You want to give up cigarettes.

You'd settle for cutting down on cigarettes.

You end up with emphysema.

You wanted to be old and benign.

You'd have settled for being old and resigned.

You end up pushing a wheelbarrow up the Fulham Road, trumpeting generalised rage and pain.

You want a long life and a gay one.

You'd settle for a long life and a contented one.

You end up living longer than you want and every time you buy a new coat you say, 'This'll see me out.'

You wanted to retire with her to a villa in Capri.

You'd have settled for spending your last days with your widowed sister in Weston-super-Mare.

You end up sleeping in a drawer in your daughter-in-law's attic.

You want to die in bed.

You'd settle for dying in your wife's arms.

You end up dying in your wife's underwear with a pimp on top of the wardrobe.

You want a state funeral.

You'd settle for a family funeral in the village church.

You end up on a slab in the morgue with a 'Who's this?' docket tied to your toe.

You wanted to clothe your neck with thunder and rejoice in your strength going on to meet the armed men, to mock fear, to swallow the ground with fierceness and rage, and say among the trumpets Ha, ha! with the thunder of the captains and the shouting.

You'd settle for rejoicing in the good of your life, eating and drinking and enjoying the fruit of all your labour.

You end up with the daughters of musick being brought low, the almond tree flourishing, the grasshopper being a burden, and desire failing, because man goeth to his long home, and the mourners go about the streets.

Picture Acknowledgments

Plate 1	Alan Davison
2	Rex Features (top), Alpha (bottom)
3	Alan Davison
4/5	Press Association
6	Jim Bennett/Alpha
7	David Parker
8	Alpha (top), Rex Features (middle), Alan Davison (bottom)

More Headline Humour:

NEVER SAY DIE

MAX HODES

Cartoons by Pete Beard

A hilarious collection of 'dying' jokes . . . Old golfers never die, they only lose their balls. Old professors never die, they only lose their faculties. Old plumbers never die, they just go round the bend . . .

Dip into this gem of a book and you'll die laughing!

NON-FICTION 0-7472-3051-X £1.95